TANGLED
HISTORY

W9-CND-276

THE WOUND IS MORTAL

The Story of the Assassination of
Abraham Lincoln

BY JESSICA GUNDERSON

Consultant:
Malcolm J. Rohrbough, PhD
Professor Emeritus, Department of History
The University of Iowa

CAPSTONE PRESS
a capstone imprint

Tangled History is published by Capstone Press,
1710 Roe Crest Drive, North Mankato, Minnesota 56003
www.capstonepub.com

Library of Congress Cataloging-in-Publication Data
Gunderson, Jessica.
The wound is mortal : the story of the assassination of Abraham Lincoln / by Jessica
Gunderson.
pages cm. —(Tangled history)
Includes bibliographical references and index.
Summary: "In a narrative nonfiction format, follows people who experienced the
events surrounding the assassination of Abraham Lincoln"— Provided by publisher.
ISBN 978-1-4914-7076-3 (library binding)
ISBN 978-1-4914-7080-0 (pbk.)
ISBN 978-1-4914-7084-8 (ebook pdf)
1. Lincoln, Abraham, 1809-1865—Assassination—Juvenile literature. I. Title.
E457.5.G86 2015
973.7092—dc23   2015010752

Editorial Credits
Adrian Vigliano, editor; Tracy Davies McCabe, designer; Tracy Cummins, media
researcher; Tori Abraham, production specialist

Photo Credits
Bridgeman Images: The Stapleton Collection, 96; Corbis: 37, 60; Getty Images:
Bob Gomel/The LIFE Picture Collection, 38, George Eastman House, 68; Library of
Congress: Cover, Cover (newspaper), 4, 6, 11, 16, 21, 24, 44; Newscom: World History
Archive, 78; Shutterstock: Picsfive, Design Element; Wikimedia: T. M. McAllister of
New York, 54.

Print in Canada.
032015   008825FRF15

TABLE OF CONTENTS

Foreword 4

1) Plots and Dreams 6

2) Surrender 16

3) "A Night We Will Never Forget" 24

4) The Stage Is Set 38

5) The Play Begins 44

6) Final Act 54

7) "The Wound Is Mortal" 60

8) "He Belongs to the Ages" 68

9) On the Killer's Trail 78

10) "I Die for My Country" 96

Farewell 105

Timeline 106

Glossary 108

Critical Thinking Using the Common Core 109

Internet Sites 109

Further Reading 110

Selected Bibliography 111

Index 112

About the Author 112

FOREWORD

By the year 1865, Americans in the North and
South had been exhausted by the war. The first election
of Abraham Lincoln back in November 1860 seemed
so long ago. Lincoln's election and opposition to the
institution of slavery had angered many Southerners.
Southern leaders were already unhappy with many U.S.
laws concerning slavery. They worried that, as president,

Lincoln would try to make slavery illegal. Seven Southern states responded to his election by seceding from the United States to form their own country called the Confederate States of America. Soon four more states joined the Confederacy. The Civil War began on April 12, 1861, when Confederate soldiers fired on Union troops in Fort Sumter, South Carolina.

Over the next four years, Lincoln had done his best to lead the Union throughout the war. But he too was exhausted, learning every day about more bloody battles. Despite the struggle, he remained committed to the preservation of the Union. In 1863 Lincoln issued the Emancipation Proclamation, which declared all slaves in the rebel states free. This worried the Confederacy even more. If the Union took control of Confederate states, all slaves in those states would be free.

When Lincoln won a second presidential term in 1864, Union forces seemed to be overpowering the Confederacy. John Wilkes Booth, the famed theatre actor and Southern sympathizer, had grown increasingly angry with Lincoln. Booth spoke openly about his love of the South and his hatred for the Union president. As the prospect of Confederate victory in the war continued to look dimmer, Booth began plotting a way that he himself might turn the tide of the war.

PLOTS AND DREAMS

1

President Abraham Lincoln

Abraham Lincoln

March 17, 1865, The White House

Someone is sobbing. The anguished cries float down the dark hallways of the White House. President Abraham Lincoln opens his eyes and listens. Could the weeping be in his mind? Perhaps echoes of the many Civil War dead? There it is again—a muffled sob.

Lincoln swings his legs over the side of the bed, stands, then steps quietly into the hallway. Moonlight shines through the windows, casting the shadow of his tall frame on the wall. The sobbing is clearer now. Louder. He feels drawn to it.

Making his way through the house, he pauses every so often to listen. *Why is there so much crying?* he wonders. *What has happened?*

He steps down the stairs, feeling almost like he is floating, and heads toward the East Room.

As he nears, the sound grows louder and seems to come from all around. He stops, unsure now how to follow the noise. Is the sound coming from above, from the sky?

A soldier steps through the door of the East Room. He looks at Lincoln. His face is blank, as though he doesn't recognize the nation's president.

Lincoln nudges past the soldier and into the East Room. Dozens of people, all in black, huddle around something in the center of the room. Their shoulders shake with sobs. *What is it?* He moves closer. A coffin.

Lincoln turns to the soldier. "Who is dead in the White House?" he asks.

"The president. He was killed by an assassin."

The president? Lincoln thinks. *But the president is me.*

He turns and moves toward the coffin. But the mourners do not move aside for him. He needs a glimpse of the body, just one glimpse—

"Mr. President? Mr. President, wake up!"

Abraham Lincoln opens his eyes to see the morning sun blazing through the curtains. His body is drenched in sweat, and his heart gallops.

A servant stands over him. "It's late," he says. "I thought it best to wake you."

"Yes, thank you," Lincoln mumbles. He rubs his eyes but can't wipe the images of the dream from his mind.

It wasn't me, he thinks. *Someone else was lying in that coffin. Not me.*

John Wilkes Booth

March 17, A restaurant in Washington, D.C.

John Wilkes Booth pours another glass of wine and stuffs an oyster in his mouth. He swallows and looks around the table at his companions.

"I have a plan, gentlemen," Booth announces in a dramatic whisper, leaning forward to look each man in the eye.

They are all here, his co-conspirators— Lewis Powell, John Surratt, Samuel Arnold, Michael O'Laughlen, David Herold, and George Atzerodt. The time has come to put his plan into action.

"Tonight, that tyrant Lincoln will be traveling to Campbell Hospital. He'll visit wounded soldiers and attend a play there," Booth says. "Tonight we will take matters into our own hands. Tonight is the night—"

"How do you know Lincoln's plans?" Arnold interrupts.

John Wilkes Booth

Booth flashes a mysterious smile. "I have my sources," he says. "As the country's most magnificent actor, I know everyone in the theatre business."

"And?" Arnold says. "What's our plan?"

Booth continues in a low voice. "It will be near dark when Lincoln leaves the hospital. We will be lying in wait for him on the darkest stretch of the road."

"And if he is guarded?" Atzerodt asks. "How will we manage then?"

Booth laughs. "The president usually travels unguarded. At most, he will have one or two soldiers with him. We can easily surprise and overpower them."

"And then?" O'Laughlen asks.

"We will hold that scoundrel for ransom in exchange for thousands of Confederate prisoners." Booth glances around the nearly empty restaurant, making sure once again that no one else is listening. He stands, his dark eyes glittering as he peers at each man around the table.

"Tonight, the South will rise again. Tonight, we will kidnap the president!"

Mary Todd Lincoln gazes out her window onto the White House lawn. The grass is turning green, leaves are budding. Tulips have pushed their way from the soil. It is spring, her favorite season. Spring is the time when everything grows, everything changes.

Except the war. The war never changes, only carries on and on with no end in sight. Abraham has told her the war is nearly won. He says the South will surrender soon, but she doesn't believe him. The last time he told her of the South's looming surrender, she cried, "The war will carry on until we are in our graves!" Abraham tried to soothe her. But she could tell he was worried. Each day Mary sees what four long years of war have done to her husband. His face, once smooth, is now torn apart by wrinkles.

Mary peers from her window and sees Abraham emerge onto the lawn. He stands still, gazing into the distance. A chill spreads through her as she thinks: *What if this is the last time I see him?* Such worries often come to her.

Mary hurries onto the lawn and to her husband's side. "I am worried for your safety," she blurts, tears swelling up. "Please be careful on your way to the hospital."

Lincoln turns to her. "Do not worry so much, my dear," he says. "I've changed my mind. I'll not be going to Campbell Hospital tonight."

John Wilkes Booth

March 17, Campbell Hospital, Washington, D.C.

Booth sighs with happiness as he gallops toward Campbell Hospital. The plan is foolproof. He and the others will overtake the president's carriage, kill the driver, capture Lincoln, and take him across the Potomac River into Virginia. Then, safely in a Southern state, they will announce the ransom—the president in exchange for Confederate prisoners.

But timing is essential. Booth has to make sure the play is on schedule.

He ties up his horse and enters the hospital in search of his actor friend, E. L. Davenport. "Hello, my friend!" Booth says, rushing toward Davenport. "Are you ready for tonight's play?"

"Certainly." Davenport smiles.

"And what of the president?"

Davenport's smile falters. "Sadly, he has changed his plans. We were so looking forward to his presence."

Booth does not wait to hear more. He whirls in fury and storms out of the hospital.

When Booth reaches the restaurant, he tells the group in a shaking voice that the president's plans have changed.

"Why?" Arnold thunders. "Was he warned? Have our plans been discovered?"

"I don't know," Booth sighs. He sinks into a chair and puts his face in his hands. "We will try again. We must try again!" he says.

When he looks up, he is alone.

SURRENDER

2

Confederate General Robert E. Lee surrendered just over a month after Lincoln's second term in office began.

Edwin Stanton

Secretary of War Edwin Stanton is jubilant. He has just received word that Confederate General Robert E. Lee has surrendered to Union General Ulysses S. Grant. With Lee's surrender, the war is nearing an end. Only a few small Confederate armies remain. Soon, Stanton knows, the others will follow Lee's example.

At the White House, Stanton hurries to the president's office, a smile on his face. When he enters, Lincoln looks at him, face haggard and ravaged. Stanton's smile drops.

"Mr. President, the war is most certainly over now. We have won! We must rejoice!"

Lincoln shakes his head. "How can I rejoice over the bodies of so many dead?"

Stanton frowns. "Our soldiers gave their lives to preserve the Union. As for the Southern rebels, let them be dead!"

Lincoln's expression doesn't change. "Those Southern rebels are our countrymen, too."

"Countrymen?" Stanton scoffs. "They are traitors."

"We must do all we can to lessen the pain of the South. They have suffered greatly."

Stanton clenches his fist and breathes in deeply, trying to control his anger. He wonders how the president can feel even a trace of sympathy for the South. The Confederate states turned against the United States. They deserve every bit of suffering they've endured. And more.

"The South must be punished," Stanton says. "The Confederate leaders should be executed for their crimes."

"Edwin, my friend," says Lincoln. "We must treat the South with grace. We must repair our country and heal these wounds."

Stanton sighs. He admires Lincoln, but he cannot agree with this attitude toward the South. "No," he mutters. "We must never forget."

Abraham Lincoln looks out over the sea of people assembled on the White House lawn. A band cheerfully plays, and fiery torches light up the night sky. Everyone is celebrating the war's end.

The crowd hushes as Lincoln steps onto the balcony overlooking the lawn. Lincoln, too, feels celebration in his heart. But he will not gloat over the victory. And, despite the gladness of the moment, he has serious matters to discuss.

"I cannot see the president!" someone cries.

Lincoln's son Tad rushes to his side with a flickering lamp. Lincoln smiles down at him. "Thank you, Tad," Lincoln murmurs. "My people can see me now."

Charles Leale

Dr. Charles Leale opens the door of the U.S. Army Hospital and takes a deep breath of fresh air. He is exhausted. Since earning his medical degree a few months ago, he has worked as a surgeon in the wounded officers' ward. His hours are long and arduous. Even though he's only 23 years old, he has seen enough suffering to last a lifetime.

"A brief walk will clear my head," Leale says aloud, beginning to wander up Pennsylvania Avenue. As he walks, he notices throngs of people heading toward the White House.

Excited, Leale wonders if the president is speaking tonight. Since the war began, Leale has been an admirer of Lincoln. He respects Lincoln's courage and honesty in handling the war and holding together the Union.

Leale follows the crowds to the White House lawn. He sees the president step onto the balcony and begin to speak. Lincoln's dark form is soon illuminated with light. As Leale listens to the president, he feels his admiration grow brighter with every word.

Dr. Charles Leale

John Wilkes Booth

John Wilkes Booth shifts his feet angrily. The crowd on the White House lawn is thick, and all around him people smile merrily and cheer. The president—that tyrant—is droning on about General Grant's victory. And worse, he's talking about ways to bring the Confederate states back into the Union.

What does he know about the Confederacy? Booth thinks. *What does he know about what the South wants?*

Booth stares up at the president, glowing in the lamplight. A perfect target. And in this crowd, no one would know the culprit.

He is jerked from his reverie by the president's next words.

"It is unsatisfactory," Lincoln says, "that the black man is not allowed to vote."

Booth cannot believe his ears. Lincoln would give freed slaves the full rights of citizens?

Booth tries to swallow the rage that rises into his throat. His mind is made up. The kidnapping plot may have failed, but a new plan—a far better plan—is emerging.

"Now, by God, I will put him through," Booth hisses. "That will be the last speech he will ever make."

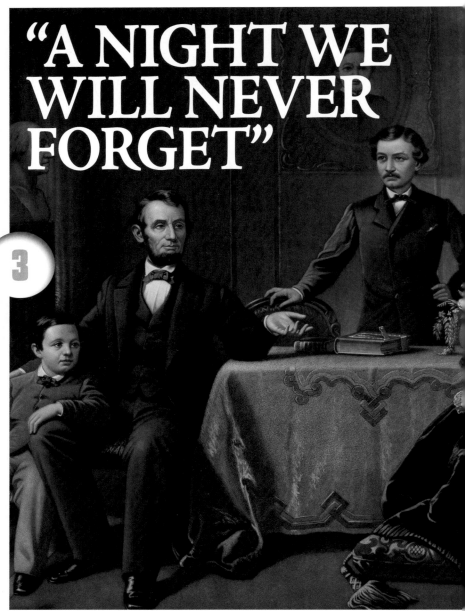

"A NIGHT WE WILL NEVER FORGET"

3

Mary Todd and Abraham were left with only their eldest son, Robert, and youngest son, Tad, after losing their middle children, Edward and William, to illnesses.

Morning light filters through the tall windows. Mary Lincoln smiles at her family gathered around the breakfast table. Abraham sits calmly while 12-year-old Tad wiggles in his chair. Their son Robert is here too, just returned from serving in the war. He was a captain on General Ulysses S. Grant's staff. Robert is 21 years old, but Mary feels as though just yesterday he was a baby.

Abraham is listening intently as Robert speaks.

"I witnessed the greatest moment of the war," Robert tells them. "The moment Lee surrendered to Grant at Appomattox."

Abraham smiles at Robert. "Tell us about it, son."

"Yes, tell us!" Tad chimes in.

All this talk of war. Mary is so very tired of the war. But the war is over now. Why spend a beautiful morning—Good Friday morning—with such talk?

"I have an idea!" Mary interrupts. "Let's go to Ford's Theatre this evening. Laura Keene is starring in *Our American Cousin*."

Abraham smiles at her. "That's a very good idea, Mary. I am in need of some entertainment. I will invite General and Mrs. Grant, too."

Mary smiles back at him. "It will be a night we'll never forget."

John Wilkes Booth

April 14, Ford's Theatre,
Washington, D.C. 10:00 a.m.

John Wilkes Booth strides into the lobby of Ford's Theatre. Familiar lines echo from the stage. The cast is practicing for tonight's performance. Booth has never starred in the comedy—he prefers dramatic roles such as those in Shakespeare. But even so, he knows *Our American Cousin* by heart and can recite every line. He pokes his head in to watch the actors. *They are good*, Booth thinks, *but I am better.*

Booth sees Harry Ford, the owner's son, and pauses to say hello. Then he wanders down the hall to pick up his mail. Along with other famous actors, he has a personal mailbox at the theatre.

He can't shake the gloom that has descended upon him. Last night, fireworks lit up the sky in celebration of Lee's surrender. But each spectacular pop seemed to pierce Booth's heart. And today, the whole city is still celebrating. Everyone except him.

Booth steps from the theatre and pauses to open his mail. Next to him, a few theatre workers are talking excitedly. He tries to ignore them, but then he hears one say, "The president and Grant are attending the play tonight!"

A flurry of hope washes Booth's gloom away. His hand trembles as he shoves his mail into his pocket. Lincoln and Grant—here, in this very theatre? *His* theatre, a place he knows inside and out.

Fate has smiled upon me, Booth thinks. *I must seize my chance!*

"Jefferson Davis must be arrested!"
Edwin Stanton thunders. "And hanged as
a traitor!"

There is silence as President Lincoln and
the other cabinet members look at him, a
few of them nodding. Stanton knows he's
not alone in his views, even though he's the
only one to speak so forcefully.

"Punishing the president of the
Confederacy is the only way to convince
the South we will not tolerate another
rebellion," Stanton continues.

Lincoln shakes his head. "I don't want
any more killing," he says.
"Enough lives have been sacrificed."

Stanton is quiet. In his opinion, the
president is too lenient with the South.
Throughout the war, he and Lincoln often

disagreed about war tactics. But Stanton is head of the War Department and the war might not have been won without his aggressive ideas. Lincoln knows this. *Perhaps he will come to his senses*, Stanton thinks.

When the meeting is over, Stanton wanders to the hall where Lincoln is speaking with General Grant. As he passes, he overhears their conversation.

"You must join us at Ford's Theatre tonight," the president tells Grant.

Grant shakes his head. "I'm afraid we can't," he says. "We are going to visit our children at their boarding school."

Stanton breaks in. "Neither of you should go to the theatre tonight." he says.

Lincoln smiles at him. "Oh, you stodgy old fellow! Would you deny me a night of entertainment, after this long war?"

"You know I don't approve of the theatre," Stanton says. "But tonight…" he breaks off. A bad feeling passes over him, but he shakes it off and bids the president goodbye. His mind has already turned back to how to deal with the South. That is more important than any theatre play.

Lincoln shuffles through the papers on his desk. He picks up one letter concerning a Union soldier awaiting execution for the crime of desertion. The author begs the president to pardon the soldier and let him live.

Lincoln quickly signs a pardon. *I know some might complain I am too lenient,* he thinks. *But I shall go to bed happy tonight as I think how joyous the signing of my name will make this young soldier, his family, and his friends.*

Lincoln signs more pardons. One is for a Confederate prisoner dying of dysentery. His family is worried he will die in prison. Lincoln signs for his release.

Finished with his paperwork, Lincoln glances at the wall clock. It is almost three o'clock. He stands and nods to his secretary. "I must go," he says. "I don't want to be late for a very important date. A carriage ride with my dear wife."

John Wilkes Booth

John Wilkes Booth leaps up the steps of Mary Surratt's boardinghouse. He can't believe his plan is finally in action. If all goes well, President Lincoln will be dead in a few hours. Three others will be dead too—General Grant, Vice President Andrew Johnson, and Secretary of State William Seward. Booth grits his teeth, determined.

Mary Surratt greets him at the door. "What is it?" she asks.

"Mary, tonight is a night we will never forget!" he tells her in a hushed voice. "But I need your help. Please send a message to your tavern in Maryland. I will arrive there this evening, and I will need guns ready for me."

Surratt frowns. "You are planning to leave Washington tonight?"

Booth nods. "Only after I have carried out my destiny." He bows dramatically as though he is on stage.

The carriage bounces along the worn road. Mary squeezes Abraham's hand, and he smiles at her.

"My dear husband," Mary says. "You almost startle me by your great cheerfulness!"

"And well I may feel so, Mary," Abraham says. "Today is the first day I feel, *really* feel, that the war has come to a close. We must be more cheerful in the future. The war has made us both very miserable."

"Yes," says Mary.

A shadow crosses Abraham's face. She wonders if he is thinking about their young son, Willie, who died three years before.

"I have a great longing to see the Pacific Ocean," Abraham says suddenly. "Will we go to see it one day, Mary?"

"Anything you wish," she murmurs, patting his shoulder.

"I see good things in our future," Abraham continues.

A shudder crawls up Mary's spine. "Please don't say such things," she says. "I fear they will bring bad luck."

Charles Leale

April 14, Armory Square Hospital, Washington, D.C., 3:00 p.m.

Dr. Charles Leale pauses to catch his breath. How many patients has he seen today? Twenty? Thirty? He can't keep track.

He continues down the hall and stops to chat with a few other doctors. He then picks up the afternoon paper and reads an announcement. Tonight President Lincoln and General Grant will be attending a play at Ford's Theatre.

"I must buy a ticket!" he exclaims. "I wouldn't miss a chance to glimpse my idol again."

John Wilkes Booth

April 14, Pennsylvania Avenue,
Washington, D.C., 4:00 p.m.

The sun is bright as John Wilkes Booth rides his horse down Pennsylvania Avenue. He fingers the gun in his pocket—a small derringer pistol. A single-shot. He has only one bullet, a single chance to kill Lincoln.

He touches the other weapon in his pocket. A knife reserved for General Grant.

Booth slows the horse and closes his eyes. He imagines the scene playing out, as he has done countless times before. At around 10:00 p.m. the funniest line of the play will be delivered. As the audience breaks into laughter, Booth will enter the president's box. First, he'll spear Grant's heart with his knife—a fitting end for a man who's caused so much bloodshed. Then, he'll spin around, whip out his pistol, and fire at Lincoln. Booth fingers the gun again. Such a small weapon to kill such a powerful tyrant! It will be like David and Goliath. Like Brutus and Caesar. He will be just as noble, just as honored, when he slays the giant.

"Hey Johnny!" a voice calls.

Booth looks up to see his friend John Matthews, a fellow actor, waving at him. He yanks the reins and dismounts, eager to see his old friend. The two men stand on the avenue chatting. John Matthews looks up as an open carriage passes. His eyes widen. "Look! There goes Grant. Looks like he's headed toward the train station."

Booth's heart lurches. Grant is on his way to the train station, not to the theatre? "Where?" he gasps.

Matthews points at the carriage, and in an instant Booth leaps onto his horse. He spurs the animal to a gallop, chasing the carriage. He has to see for himself.

As he nears the carriage, he slows and peers in. Sure enough, it's General and Mrs. Grant.

When Grant glances up, Booth gives him a cold look—a look that could kill.

President Lincoln helps Mary from the carriage. "What a wonderful afternoon!" he says, grinning. Turning to escort her to the White House, he sees two familiar figures walking down the lawn. It's Illinois Governor Richard Oglesby and General Isham Haynie. He waves and rushes to them.

"Come inside," he says.

Lincoln leads the two men to the reception room. He doesn't want to talk business. Not today. Instead, he opens a favorite book of political humor. "Let me read to you," he says. "And let us laugh!"

When the butler announces it's time for dinner, Lincoln nods. "Just a few more minutes!" he says. He's having too much fun to stop now. Finally, after repeated urgings from the butler, Lincoln closes the book. "Well, friends, our fun must now end. Until next time!"

The White House, 1865

THE STAGE IS SET

4

Theatre staff prepared a special box for the president's party by adding flags, portraits, and special furniture such as a rocking chair and sofa.

John Wilkes Booth

John Wilkes Booth makes his way through the dark theatre. All is quiet now, but in a few hours the seats will be filled with people ready to see *Our American Cousin*. But they will have no idea what's really in store for them. It will be the drama of the century, played out before their eyes.

But Booth has one final preparation to make. He searches backstage and finds what he's looking for—the wooden back of a music stand. With the piece of wood in hand, he heads to the presidential box.

The box has an outer door and an inner door. With his knife, Booth gouges a hole just inside the outer door. After he enters the box tonight, he'll wedge the music stand into the hole, barring the door against anyone who tries to come in. Then he'll be free to carry out his attack.

Mary Lincoln's head hurts. Perhaps it's from the bouncing carriage ride. Perhaps it's from the brilliant sun. Or it could be from the long, exhausting war.

She takes a sip of water and looks across the table at her husband. "I am not sure I feel well enough for the theatre tonight," she tells him.

"Oh, Mary," Abraham says. "But we must go! I am in desperate need of some relaxation."

"I know you are. But … "

"And what of Clara Harris and Henry Rathbone? The friends who are to accompany us?"

Mary nods. "Yes, of course. We must not let them down. We will go."

She shivers and takes another sip of water.

Edwin Stanton

Secretary of War Edwin Stanton has had a long day, but he cannot return home until he calls on his friend, Secretary of State William Seward. A few weeks earlier, Seward was in a serious carriage accident and is still in bed, recovering.

Seward smiles when Stanton enters the room. "Tell me about the cabinet meeting today," he says.

Stanton recounts the day's events. "We must figure a way to deal with the South," he concludes. "But tonight we can rest easy. The war is over."

When Stanton returns home, he finds a gathering outside his house. The crowd breaks into song, cheering him for his role in the Union victory.

Stanton bows and waves. Yes, he will rest easy tonight.

John Wilkes Booth

"Where is George?" John Wilkes Booth thunders. He looks at the clock above the bed in Lewis Powell's small rented room. George Atzerodt is late for this meeting— one Booth considers very important.

"Go to his hotel and fetch him," Booth orders Powell.

After Powell leaves, Booth turns to David Herold. "He'd better not be backing out," he mutters.

Herold shrugs.

Powell soon returns with a shaking Atzerodt in tow. At last the four conspirators are all here to go over the final plan.

"Powell, at 10:00 p.m., you and Herold will go to Secretary Seward's home.

Tell whoever opens the door that you are delivering medicine. Then go to Seward's room and kill him. Herold will wait outside with your getaway horse."

Powell and Herold nod. "I'm ready," Powell says.

"And George, you will kill Vice President Johnson in his hotel room at 10:00 p.m. After the deeds are done, we will all meet at Soper's Hill outside of D.C."

"I do not want to do it," Atzerodt blurts.

Booth glares at him. "It's too late to back out now," he growls. "The stage is set. The actors are in motion. Let the curtains open, and let us hear the applause!"

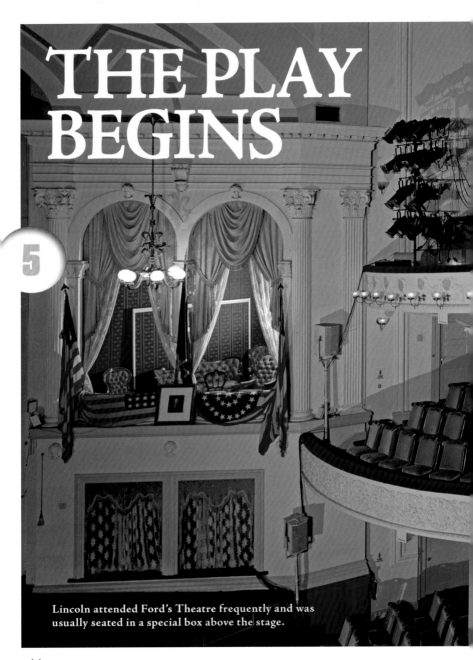

THE PLAY BEGINS

5

Lincoln attended Ford's Theatre frequently and was usually seated in a special box above the stage.

Mary Todd Lincoln

April 14, Washington, D.C., 8:20 p.m.

"We are late," Mary Lincoln says as their carriage arrives in front of the Harris home.

"I'm sure Clara and Henry will forgive us," Abraham assures her. "And we won't miss too much of the play."

Mary smiles at Clara and Henry as they climb into the carriage.

"What a beautiful night!" Clara says. "Thank you for inviting us."

Henry clears his throat and looks at Abraham. "Mr. President, I must ask. Why isn't the cavalry accompanying you?"

Abraham shrugs. "I do not allow guards to accompany me to church or to the theatre. I like to feel like a regular human being sometimes."

Mary glances down and sees that Abraham is not wearing his gloves.

45

It is not proper to be in public without gloves, she thinks. She is about to chide him but stops herself. Why spoil the evening with a bit of nagging? This is her husband's night to enjoy himself.

Mary Lincoln squeezes her husband's hand. *Could our troubles finally be over?* she wonders. She sneaks a glance at him. He is more cheerful today than she has seen in years. Her headache is gone now. She's glad they decided to attend the play. Abraham needs this night of enjoyment. They both do.

Charles Leale

April 14, Ford's Theatre, 8:25 p.m.

From his theatre seat, Dr. Charles Leale glances up again at the presidential box, draped in flags and decorations. The president has not yet arrived, but soon Leale will get a get a glimpse of his hero.

Leale is entranced by the play. He's never been much of a theatregoer, but he finds himself enjoying the humor and the acting.

Suddenly, the main actress, Laura Keene, stops speaking. She smiles into the audience and begins to clap.

Leale turns to look. President Lincoln enters the theatre. The doctor leaps to his feet and applauds along with others around him. The orchestra strikes up "Hail to the Chief," the official presidential anthem of the United States.

Leale, along with more than 1,600 theatregoers, watches as the president makes his way to the balcony, waves and bows, then takes his seat.

After the crowd settles, Leale turns his eyes back to the stage, feeling satisfied at his glimpse of the president.

Lights from the theatre glow onto the dark alley. John Wilkes Booth leads his horse to the back door, where he spots his friend, a theatre worker named Ed Spangler. "Hold my horse for a while?" Booth asks.

Spangler shakes his head. "I'm too busy with stage props," he says. "But John Peanuts can help you."

Booth tosses the reins to Peanuts and then hurries inside. He pauses to listen as the actors speak their lines. Timing is everything, and he has to be sure.

Harry Hawk, the main actor, blurts a few words. Booth knows exactly which scene of the play is happening. He has one hour until Hawk utters the fateful line that will make the audience laugh and drown out the gunshot. One hour.

First, though, Booth needs to get to the other side of the theatre and exit through the side door. Then he will enter the theatre through the front door. That way, everyone will think he came on foot down Tenth Street, and no one will suspect he has a getaway horse out back. Once the deed is done, he can jump to the stage, rush out the back door, and gallop away.

Glancing around to make sure no one is watching, Booth kneels and tugs open a trapdoor. *He slides his feet through the hole and jumps, plunging into darkness.*

Now he can't even see his hands in front of his face. Carefully he makes his way forward, touching the dirt wall for guidance. The tunnel runs below the stage to the other side.

A spider web brushes against his face, and Booth irritably wipes it away. He can't come out of the tunnel looking dirty and disheveled—that might arouse suspicion. He needs to look normal.

At last, he stumbles upon the steps leading out of the tunnel. He runs up the steps, through the door, and out of the darkness. He is just to the right of the stage now. Murmurs and laughter from the crowd greet him.

The president is so close.

But it's not time yet. He has to wait.

Booth slips through a side door into the alley. His throat is dry, and his heart hammering. He needs something to calm his nerves. Taltavul's Saloon is just next door.

Booth brushes off his jacket, runs a hand through his hair, and marches into the dim, smoky saloon.

"Hello, John," the owner greets him.

"Whiskey and water," Booth says. His voice sounds like a croaking frog, but Taltavul doesn't seem to notice. He slides Booth's drink across the counter. Booth swallows the whiskey in one gulp and checks the clock.

It's almost time.

In the presidential box Lincoln takes a seat at the high-backed rocking chair placed there for him. He feels so happy, sitting here in the theatre with his wife and friends. *Our American Cousin* is one of his favorite plays. He can relate to the main character, a rough, backwoods American with no manners visiting high-society England. Lincoln himself has been called a crude backwoodsman. Some people have accused him of having no manners or grace. But Lincoln knows that even though he doesn't have the polished manners of many in Washington, D.C., he's honest and hardworking. He's done the best he can as president in these tough war times.

He smiles at a line in the play and takes his wife's hand.

"What will Miss Harris think of my holding onto you so?" Mary whispers.

"She will think nothing of it," Lincoln assures her.
He doesn't realize these are the last words he will
ever speak.

John Buckingham
April 14, Ford's Theatre, 9:59 p.m.

John Buckingham, a doorkeeper at Ford's
Theatre, sighs as the front door of the theatre opens.
It has been a long night. The theatre is packed
because of the president's visit. All evening people
have been begging for tickets, but there are no tickets
left. Every seat is taken.

Buckingham is ready to tell whoever just entered
that there are no tickets left, but when he looks
up, he sees it is not a patron at all. It's John Wilkes
Booth, an actor he knows well.

"Hello, Johnny!" says Buckingham.

Booth barely glances at him. He seems like he's in
a hurry. "Please, tell me the time!" Booth demands.

How does Booth not know the time? Buckingham
thinks. *The clock is on the wall, where it's always been.*

Buckingham gestures to the clock. Booth peers at it and nods, then scurries into the theatre. Buckingham looks after him, shrugs, and returns to his work.

John Wilkes Booth
April 14, Ford's Theatre, 10:05 p.m.

Booth brushes past spectators and mounts the winding staircase leading to the balcony level. He's glad to see a full theatre. He loves playing to a packed house.

At the top of the stairs he pauses to watch the action on stage. A few heads turn his way, and he hears his name whispered. He knows the spectators recognize him. *All the better*, he thinks. *I would not want any doubt as to my identity.*

He doesn't need to check the clock. The moment is almost upon him.

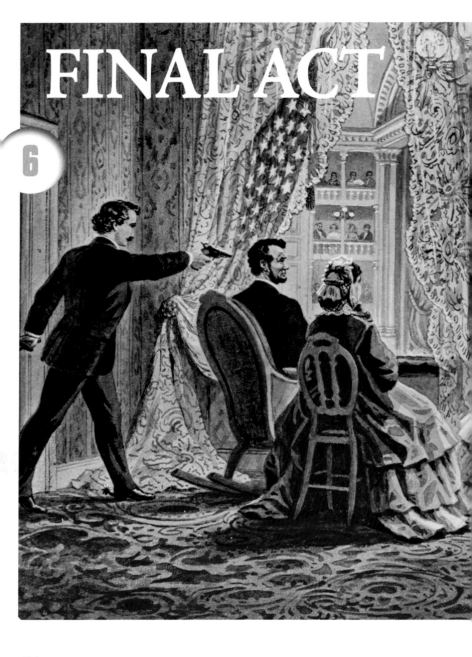

FINAL ACT

6

April 14, Ford's Theatre, 10:10 p.m.

A man sits outside the door to the president's box. As Booth comes closer, he realizes it is the president's valet rather than an armed guard. A stroke of luck!

The valet looks up as Booth approaches. Booth pulls out a calling card with his name on it and hands it to the valet. The valet peers at the card, then looks Booth over. Booth sees a spark of recognition in his eyes, and then the valet nods for him to enter.

Once inside, Booth grabs the block of wood he'd placed there earlier and wedges the door shut.

Now no one else can enter.

Abraham Lincoln gazes around the theatre. *These are my fellow countrymen,* he thinks. *Here we are, gathered together like friends. No matter our political beliefs. For a few hours, we can put aside our differences and enjoy the play.*

Lincoln spots some familiar faces in the crowd and leans forward to nod. Then he turns his attention to the stage. "You are not used to the manners of good society!" one of the characters yells. Lincoln smiles.

Booth peers through the peephole into the presidential box. Lincoln sits in a high-backed rocking chair. Booth watches as the president leans forward to acknowledge someone in the crowd.

He is close, so close Booth can see every whisker on his cheek, every wrinkle on his face.

Quietly, Booth nudges the door open. He pulls the derringer pistol from his pocket and cocks the hammer.

Onstage, Harry Hawk is about to speak.

The president grins as the characters exit the stage, leaving Harry Hawk alone. Hawk gestures wildly. "Don't know the manners of good society, eh?" he says. "Well, I guess I know enough to turn you inside out, old gal; you sockdologizing old man-trap!"

Lincoln bursts into laughter along with the crowd.

The theatre thunders with laughter.
Booth aims the gun at the back of Lincoln's head.
Then he pulls the trigger.

Mary chuckles as the audience roars with laughter. The smile has barely left her lips when suddenly Abraham slumps forward. Alarmed, she catches him, thinking he has fainted.

Then the distinct smell of gunpowder reaches her nostrils.

She screams the loudest scream of her life.

I've done it! Booth thinks as he lunges forward.

He aims to jump over the balcony, but someone is in his way. It's Henry Rathbone, the president's companion.

Booth has no more bullets, but he does have his knife. As Rathbone tackles him, Booth stabs the man with all his might.

Rathbone gasps in pain and falls backward. Blood spurts from the wound, spraying the presidential box with blood.

Booth leaps over the railing to the stage below.

Her husband has been shot. Her dear Abraham! Mary holds his head in her lap, sobbing and screaming at the same time.

She hears a thud as the assassin drops to the stage. "Stop him!" she screams. *"Stop that man!"*

Something snaps as Booth hits the stage. Fierce pain clamps over his left ankle. Wincing, he delivers his final line onstage. *"Sic semper tyrannis!"* he cries to the confused crowd. "Thus always to tyrants!"

Dr. Leale sees a man drop onto the stage. His face is familiar. *Is it John Wilkes Booth, the famous actor?* he wonders. *Is this part of the play?*

But the actor is shouting something about tyrants, something that makes no sense.

Then, in a split second, he hears the screams. He turns to see a blue cloud of smoke drifting above the presidential box. Leale knows then that his life will never be the same, for this grand theatre has turned into a battlefield.

Booth shoves past a shocked Harry Hawk and races backstage. He can hear the audience shouting his name. Or are they cheering?

He pushes open the back door. John Peanuts is still holding his horse. He looks like he may have been sleeping. He blinks at Booth.

Booth can't risk having Peanuts detain him. He whacks Peanuts on the side of the head with his pistol, leaps onto the horse, and gallops away into the night.

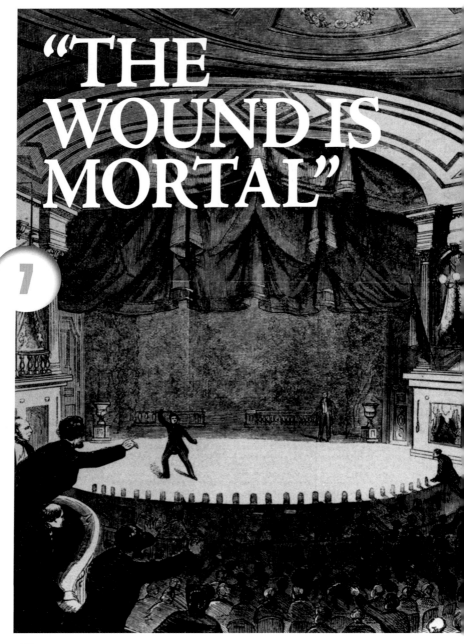

"THE WOUND IS MORTAL"

7

Charles Leale,

Dr. Leale shoves his way through the crowd outside the presidential box. "I'm a doctor!" he shouts. "Let me pass!"

He reaches the door and pushes against it. It won't budge. Something is holding the door shut.

With his shoulder, he lunges against the door again and again. Then he hears a voice from inside.

"Wait!" cries the voice.

Finally the door opens and Leale sees a blood-soaked man holding a long piece of wood. "He blocked the door," the man gasps. "Please help me. I've been stabbed."

With one look, Leale knows the man is not fatally wounded. He pushes past him into the presidential box.

President Lincoln lies in the arms of the First Lady.

"Please move aside," Leale tells her. "I'm a surgeon."

Leale kneels over the president and discovers he's still breathing. With a pocketknife he rips open Lincoln's collar to find the bullet wound.

His heart sinks. The president has been shot in the head. There's no saving him.

He swallows and looks at the First Lady. "I'm sorry," he says. "The wound is mortal."

John Wilkes Booth

April 14, Eleventh Street, Washington, D.C., 10:35 p.m.

The horse's hoofbeats echo into the quiet night. No one is following him. Booth smiles with satisfaction. He has escaped!

At the Eleventh Street Bridge leading out of Washington, Booth slows his horse. A guard steps onto the bridge.

"Stop, sir!" the guard says. "No one's allowed to leave Washington this late at night. What is your business?"

"I'm on my way home to Maryland," Booth tells him.

"And what is your name?"

Booth straightens and looks the guard in the eye. "My name is John Wilkes Booth."

The guard looks him over and nods. "I'll let you pass," he says. "But you cannot return until morning."

Booth smiles. "I have no intention of returning. Not ever."

Edwin Stanton

April 14, Washington, D.C., 10:30 p.m.

"William Seward has been murdered!"

Secretary of War Edwin Stanton jumps from bed at his wife's scream from downstairs. He rubs his eyes. Seward? Murdered?

Stanton pulls on his clothes and rushes downstairs. A red-faced messenger stands panting at the door. "Someone murdered William Seward!" the messenger exclaims.

"I must go," Stanton says. He grabs his hat and rushes into the night.

John Wilkes Booth

Soper's Hill rises in front of him. Booth spurs his exhausted horse up the hill, glancing behind him to make sure he's not being followed. The meeting place under the oak tree is empty. The others haven't arrived. Booth reins in his horse under the shadows of the tree and waits. Hopefully the others carried out their end of the deal. His leg aches, and he's thirsty. But in some ways he's never felt better.

Hoofbeats break the silence of the night. Someone is coming. Booth peers through the trees and sees David Herold riding alone up the hill.

"Herold!" Booth calls. "Over here."

Breathless, Herold rides toward him.

"Where are the others?" Booth demands. "And what of Seward? Is he dead?"

"I think so," Herold says, catching his breath. "Powell went into the house, and I waited outside, like you told me. Then I heard screams coming from inside. Seward's daughter opened the window and shouted that her father was murdered. I couldn't wait for Powell. I had to take off before I was discovered."

Booth smiles. Everything is going according to plan. "And what about Atzerodt? Did he kill the vice president?"

"I don't know," Herold tells him.

"We can't wait for them," Booth says. He nudges his horse with his boot, and the two men gallop toward Surratt's tavern.

Lights blaze in the windows of Seward's home. "Here! Stop here!" Stanton tells the driver. He jumps from the carriage just as another one pulls up. Gideon Welles, another member of the president's cabinet, exits the other carriage.

"Have you heard?" Welles shouts to him. "Seward has been murdered and the president has been shot!"

A cold chill creeps up Stanton's spine. "Both of them? Tonight?"

Welles grasps Stanton's arm. "No one is safe," he says.

"Danger lurks everywhere."

The two men push through the crowd outside the house and enter Seward's home. Stanton gasps at what he sees inside. Blood is everywhere, dripping from the stairs, smearing the walls, pooling on the landing.

Stanton has never seen so much blood. "A massacre," he whispers.

Stanton looks up to see Fanny, Seward's daughter, shivering and crying at the top of the stairs. He rushes to her. "Your father … is he dead?"

Fanny shakes her head. "No. He managed to survive, though he's wounded badly. A doctor is tending to him now."

"What happened?"

"A man came in … said he had medicine. Then he barged his way upstairs, stabbing everyone he saw. Five people … my brother too."

"No one is dead?"

"No," Fanny whispers.

"Where is the attacker?"

"He got away," Fanny says.

Stanton looks at Welles.

"What does this mean?" Welles says. "A conspiracy to kill us all?"

"We must go to the president," Stanton tells him. "Despite the danger."

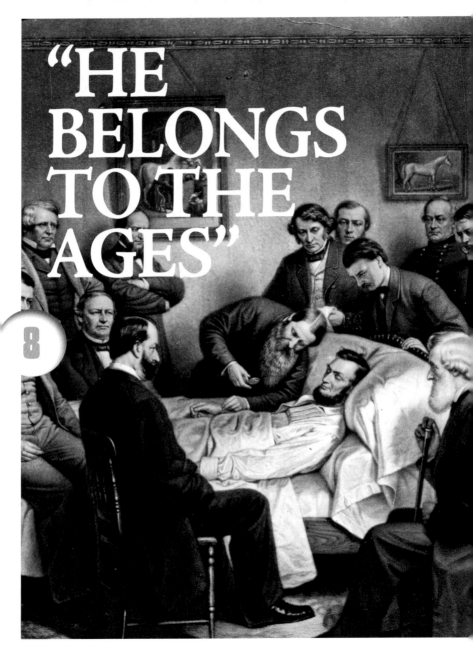

"HE BELONGS TO THE AGES"

8

Mary Todd Lincoln

In a rear bedroom of the Petersen boardinghouse, President Lincoln lies on the small bed. Dr. Leale and others carried him from the theatre to the nearest house, afraid he wouldn't survive a trip to the hospital. The president takes jagged, raspy breaths as Mary Lincoln runs her hand over his hair. Tears stream down her face.

Grief overwhelms her. Here is a man who has stood by her through tough times. He has protected her and cared for her. And now she will be alone.

Doctor Leale touches her shoulder. "I am sorry, Mrs. Lincoln," he says gently. "You must go while I examine the president."

Mary nods. On wobbling legs she moves to the front parlor, where her son, Robert, catches her as she starts to faint.

Edwin Stanton

Edwin Stanton marches into the rear bedroom where the president lies gasping for breath. With a sinking heart, Stanton realizes Lincoln is close to death.

Stanton will not leave the nation leaderless. Times like these require action. He leaves the room and heads for the rear parlor, where he takes a seat at a small table.

One of his colleagues approaches him. "What will we do, Secretary Stanton?"

Stanton gives him a solid nod. "I will take on the role of president," he says. "And I will find the culprits and bring them to justice. Bring me my first witness."

John Wilkes Booth

April 15, Surratt's tavern,
Surrattsville, Maryland, 12:15 a.m.

Surratt's tavern is dark. Booth slumps against his horse's sweaty neck as David Herold leaps up the front steps. He pounds hard on the wooden door, once, twice, three times. Finally the door swings open and Lloyd, the tavern keeper, blinks at them. Herold shoves his way inside and grabs a bottle of whiskey. "Get us those things Mrs. Surratt brought you!" he tells Lloyd. "Hurry!"

Lloyd disappears up the stairs and Herold brings the whiskey to Booth. "Drink. It'll help with the pain."

Booth takes a large gulp that burns his throat. Lloyd steps from the house with two guns and a field glass. Herold grabs one of the guns, but Booth refuses the other. "I can't hold onto it. My leg ... I need both hands to hold to my horse."

Herold leaps onto his horse and heads toward the road. Booth starts to follow, then pauses and looks down at Lloyd. "Let me tell you some news," he says. "I am pretty certain we have assassinated the president and Secretary Seward."

Charles Leale

April 15, Petersen boardinghouse, 3:30 a.m.

Dr. Leale collapses onto a chair next to the president's bed. Lincoln's pulse is becoming weaker and his breaths more staggered. The sky is lightening with coming dawn. Leale cannot believe the president has managed to live this long. But his death is near, Leale is certain.

Edwin Stanton

Edwin Stanton rubs his eyes. He has heard testimony from six witnesses from Ford's Theatre. All witnesses have identified the shooter as John Wilkes Booth.

Before interviewing any witnesses, Stanton ordered bridges closed, trains searched, roads patrolled. He sent warnings to the president's cabinet, believing them all to be in danger. He also ordered General Grant to return to Washington.

Stanton's colleagues think he should've called for John Wilkes Booth's arrest right away. But Stanton is a thorough man. He has to be absolutely sure.

And now, hours later, Stanton is sure. He sends out a telegram naming John Wilkes Booth, the famous, beloved actor, as the assassin.

John Wilkes Booth

"Open up! Dr. Mudd, open up!" David Herold raps frantically on the door.

Booth shivers under his thick shawl. Overhead, the moon is swinging toward the horizon. Dawn will be here soon. The horse shifts and Booth's leg screams in pain at the movement. More than anything, he needs to rest. At last, a man in a long nightshirt, candle in hand, swings open the door.

"My friend is hurt," Herold blurts. "Please help."

Dr. Mudd gazes at Booth. They've met before, both Confederate sympathizers, but Booth can't tell if Mudd recognizes him. Finally Mudd nods. Booth dismounts and hobbles into the doctor's home.

With one look, Dr. Mudd declares Booth's leg broken.

Mudd and Herold help Booth up the stairs to a bedroom. Mudd slices open Booth's boot, removes it from his foot, and sets the bone. He uses pieces of a hatbox as a splint. "Now, boy, you need to rest," Mudd tells Booth. He glances at Herold, who's leaning against the doorframe, exhausted. "You both need to rest. You may stay here."

Charles Leale

April 15, Petersen boardinghouse, 7:00 a.m.

Lincoln's end is near. Dr. Leale knows each breath might be the president's last. Just before 7:00 a.m., he sends for Mary Lincoln so she can say a final goodbye to her husband.

After a distraught Mary leaves the room, Dr. Leale and two other doctors use their fingers to feel the president's slow pulse. For nearly a minute, Leale feels no surge of pulse. Lincoln's breathing stops. At 7:22 a.m. Lincoln's heart beats one last time. The three doctors look at each other. The end has arrived.

One of the doctors crosses Lincoln's hands over his chest. "He is gone," the doctor says. "He is dead."

Everyone in the room is silent, mourning the death of their leader. Lincoln's pastor, who has been called to his bedside, murmurs a quick prayer. Secretary Edwin Stanton, tears streaming down his cheeks, says in a shaking voice, "Now he belongs to the ages."

Dr. Leale bows his head. He came to the theatre tonight to see his hero, Lincoln. And now he's seen more than he ever wished.

John Wilkes Booth

April 15, Home of Dr. Samuel Mudd, 5:00 p.m.

For nearly twelve hours Booth has drifted in and out of sleep, his dreams filled with gunshots and applause. Now Herold is shaking him awake.

"Booth! We gotta get out of here. The cavalry is combing the country, looking for us!"

Booth can't help but smile. He reaches to touch his moustache, then remembers he shaved it off this morning.

"How do you know?" he asks.

"Doc and I went to town to find us a buggy. When we reached the edge of town, I saw Yankee soldiers everywhere! I left Dr. Mudd in town and returned here immediately."

Booth stretches and looks out the window. The sun is close to setting. If they wait awhile, they can make their escape under the cover of night.

"We gotta leave now!" Herold urges. "What if Dr. Mudd betrays us?"

Booth leans back against his pillow. "I'll take my chances," he says.

SURRAT.

BOOTH.

HAROLD.

War Department, Washington, April 20, 1865,

9

$100,000 REWARD!

THE MURDERER

Of our late beloved President, Abraham Lincoln,

IS STILL AT LARGE.

ON THE KILLER'S TRAIL

Dr. Mudd returns from town, distraught and agitated.

"I heard some news in town," he says, eyeing Booth carefully. "Lincoln is dead. Shot by an assassin who is still on the loose."

"Terrible news," Booth mutters sarcastically, catching Mudd's eye. "And did you tell anyone that you are harboring two suspicious men?"

Mudd grunts. "You both need to get out of my house."

"We need to cross the Potomac River into Virginia," Booth says. "Can you tell us the way?"

Mudd nods. "I know a man named Samuel Cox. He will help you." Mudd pauses and frowns at Booth's broken leg. "And, I know a doctor in Virginia named Richard Stuart. He will help you, too."

Edwin Stanton

Edwin Stanton will not rest until every last conspirator is jailed. He orders that Ford's Theatre be thoroughly examined and investigated. And he orders the arrest of anyone associated with the theatre or John Wilkes Booth.

John Wilkes Booth. The name strikes anger in Stanton's heart. Where is he? Soldiers and detectives have been scouring the countryside for two days. No sign of Booth. Only false leads. And Stanton still knows nothing about Seward's attacker, not even a name.

On the third day, Monday, April 17, Stanton finally has a stroke of luck. Detectives arrived at Mary Surratt's boardinghouse to question her, since she was a known friend of Booth. While they were questioning her, Lewis Powell happened to wander in. When he saw the detectives, Powell backed away. "Wrong house," he muttered.

Powell's words aroused the detectives' suspicions. They interrogated him as to his whereabouts since April 14. Then they sent for Secretary Seward's doorman, William Bell.

When Bell saw Powell, he gasped.

"That's the man that cut Master Seward!"

The detectives arrested Powell and Mary Surratt immediately. That same day Samuel Arnold and Michael O'Laughlen, participants in Booth's original kidnapping plot, are arrested as well. Stanton is making headway. But he is far from satisfied. Booth must be found.

John Wilkes Booth

John Wilkes Booth shivers under the flimsy, damp blanket. He is dirty, tired, and hungry. The chilly night air smells of rain.

"I wish we could light a fire," Herold mumbles.

Booth doesn't answer. Both men know a fire is out of the question. Soldiers are combing the area. They can't risk being spotted.

Booth breathes deeply. The Potomac River is so close he can smell it. And so is Virginia. And freedom. As Dr. Mudd promised, Samuel Cox helped them. Cox's friend, Tom Jones, is willing to give them a boat to cross the river. But first, they have to wait for a dark night. According to Jones, soldiers are all around the area. Jones persuaded Booth and Herold to hunker down and wait. So here they are, in a pine thicket, stuck in the cold.

Worse, Jones has brought Booth newspaper accounts of the assassination. The newspapers call Booth a coward and a criminal. Even Southern newspapers criticize his act. Booth is shocked. This is not what he imagined. He wanted to be a hero. Now, in his dirt-smeared clothes, nursing an aching, broken leg, he feels like nothing but a common fugitive.

On the night of April 20, Booth and Herold steer a small boat across the Potomac River. They keep as quiet as possible under cover of the pitch-black night. No stars twinkle above them.

Suddenly, a shape looms in front of them. "A Union gunboat!" Booth hisses.

Frantically, Herold rows away from the ship, against the current. At last, in the waning darkness, Herold spots a familiar landmark. "Blossom Point," he says, pointing. "I know this area. And I know some folks who'll help us."

"Excellent!" Booth exclaims.

"Yeah," Herold mumbles. "But there's a problem. We must've got turned around. We're back in Maryland. Not Virginia."

Lieutenant Alexander Lovett peers intently at the man in front of him. Something is not right. The man, Dr. Mudd, seems fidgety. He doesn't seem to want to answer Lovett's questions. "Tell me again about the two men who came here for help," Lovett says.

Mudd hurriedly describes the men. "They were strangers," he says. "I didn't know either of them until they knocked on my door," he says.

"But you do know John Wilkes Booth?" Lovett asks.

Mudd nods. "I met him once, last fall."

Colonel Henry Wells slides a photograph toward Mudd. "Is this the man who came to your home?" he demands.

Mudd stares at the picture of Booth. Lovett thinks he can see the doctor's mind racing. Finally Mudd looks up from the picture. "Yes," he says. "I didn't realize it was him.

This is the stranger you are looking for."

Wells turns to Lovett with a nod. "We must send word to Stanton," he says. "We are on the killer's trail."

John Wilkes Booth
April 23, Banks of Potomac River, Virginia

Virginia at last! Booth leans against the tree and stares at the rising sun. The Potomac River splashes near him. Minutes pass, then hours. *Herold is taking too long,* Booth thinks.

They wasted another night in Maryland with Herold's friends until finally rowing across the Potomac. When they landed in Virginia, Herold set off on foot to the home of Elizabeth Quesenberry, a staunch Confederate who would help them. Booth stayed behind, hidden near the river. With his injured leg, he couldn't bear a long walk.

Booth hears rustling in the trees. Herold appears with two horses and a bundle of food. Booth's stomach growls.

"Where are we going next?" Herold asks, swinging onto his horse.

"Dr. Richard Stuart's," Booth says. "Perhaps he will show us some fine Southern hospitality."

When they reach Stuart's home, Herold does the talking. "We are Confederate soldiers," Herold tells the doctor. "My brother here, James Boyd, is badly injured. Will you put us up for the night?"

Booth watches Dr. Stuart's reaction. Stuart hesitates before answering. "I will give you food, but that is all. After that, you'd best be on your way."

Booth can scarcely hide his anger throughout the meal. Yes, Dr. Stuart has allowed them to eat at his fine table, even though they are dirty and bedraggled. But he has also been downright rude. Is this any way to treat a wounded soldier?

After the meal, Stuart hurries them out the door. "You might be able to rent a wagon from William Lucas, a free black who lives near," he tells them.

They find Lucas' home, but he has nothing to offer. "I got a full house here, with my wife and six children all in this little cabin. No room for the two of you."

Rage floods Booth's body. Here they are in Confederate Virginia and no one will help them. Booth reaches into his back pocket and whips out a Bowie knife.

Lucas steps back as Booth waves the knife in his face. "We'll be sleeping in your cabin tonight, do you hear?" Booth spits.

Lucas gives him a frightened nod and ushers the men inside.

Edwin Stanton
April 24, Washington, D.C.

Edwin Stanton's heart leaps at the information from Colonel Wells and Lieutenant Lovett. First of all, they've discovered Booth has a broken leg. And he has shaved his moustache. Most importantly the investigators believe that Booth and Herold are almost certainly headed to Virginia.

Stanton makes a decision. He will send the New York Sixteenth Cavalry to Virginia, led by Luther Baker, Edward Doherty, and Everton Conger.

John Wilkes Booth

Morning sunlight glints on the waves of the Rappahannock River. "Here you are," William Lucas' son Charley pulls on the reins of the horse and stops the wagon. "Port Conway. You can take a ferry across the river."

Herold helps Booth from the wagon and the two men look around.

As the wagon moves away, Booth sees the ferry. Gloom descends upon him. The ferry is on the other side of the river. And no one is in sight. He sinks his aching body onto a pier.

"Halloo!" Herold calls. "Anyone around?"

A man emerges and steps up the riverbank toward them. "I'm Rollins. What do you need?"

Herold tells Rollins they are Confederate soldiers returning home. "We need to get across the river."

"I can take you across. But first I gotta set out my fishing nets."

"Guess we have to wait," Herold mutters and slumps down next to Booth.

After a few minutes, Booth hears an unmistakable sound: hoofbeats, moving quickly toward the river.

Herold grabs Booth's arm. "Soldiers!" he hisses.

Everton Conger
April 24, Virginia

Everton Conger has seen it all—long years in the war, wounded three times in battle—but this might be his most daring mission yet. He and 25 soldiers have just arrived in Virginia. They are heading deep into enemy territory, in search of a killer.

Conger mounts his horse. The old wound in his hip aches, but it's nothing he can't handle. He's strong and determined. And he won't rest until he catches Lincoln's killer.

"All right, boys!" he calls. "Onward into Virginia!"

With the thunder of hooves behind him, Conger leads the way through Virginia. At every house, every farm, the cavalrymen pound on doors and demand cooperation.

"Have you seen this man?" they demand, shoving a photo of Booth into scared people's faces.

The cavalry spreads wide, traveling south toward Port Conway and the Rappahannock River.

John Wilkes Booth
April 24, Port Conway, Virginia

Confederates! Booth heaves a sigh of relief when he sees the soldiers' uniforms. They aren't Union cavalry out to get him. In fact, they may help him.

Herold approaches the three soldiers. Booth expects to hear the old made-up story about him being a wounded Confederate soldier. But instead he hears Herold say, "See that man over there? He's the assassin of Abraham Lincoln!"

One soldier gazes at Booth in awe. "Wow!" he says. "A hero. Wish I could've done the same."

Booth smiles. *At last!*

"My name's Willie Jett, and I'm from around these parts," the young soldier says. "I know just the place to take you. Richard Garrett's farm.

Only you gotta pretend you're just a wounded soldier on your way home."

"I can do that," Booth grins.

Everton Conger

April 25, Port Conway, Virginia

Everton Conger glares into the face of William Rollins. "You helped two men cross the river," Conger says. "Who were they?"

"There were five men," Rollins says in a trembling voice. "Confederate soldiers. So they said."

Five men! Conger raises his eyebrows. This is a new development.

"Did you know any of the men?"

Rollins nods. "Just young Willie Jett."

"Did any of them have a broken leg?"

"Yes."

Luther Baker brings out a photograph of Booth. "Is this the man?"

Rollins stares at the picture, his eyes wide.

"That's him. Except he didn't have a moustache."

"Tell me," Conger demands. "Where can I find Willie Jett?"

"Likely at the Star Hotel," Rollins says. "In the town of Bowling Green, across the river."

Conger calls for the troops to join him on the riverbank. "Well, then, Rollins. Ferry us across."

John Wilkes Booth

April 25, Garrett Farm,
near Bowling Green, Virginia

Booth stretches lazily in his bed at the Garrett farm. For the first time in ten days, he's had a good night's sleep. He rises from bed, grabs his crutches, and hobbles into the front room.

Richard Garrett's grandchildren greet him excitedly. It seems they are happy to have a mysterious, wounded soldier in their midst. And Booth is happy to entertain them. Here is a stage he can act upon. He grins at the children and takes on the role of James W. Boyd, wounded Confederate soldier.

The good mood is spoiled some time later when two men on horseback charge down the lane toward the Garrett farm. Booth rises from his spot on the porch, where he's been relaxing. He sees that the men are the other two soldiers who accompanied Willie Jett the day before.

"Union soldiers everywhere!" one of the riders gasps. "Comin' this way!"

The two soldiers wheel their horses about and gallop away. Booth's heart is beating as fast as the horses' hooves. "I think we'd best head toward the woods," Booth suggests to Herold. He limps off the porch as fast as he can, and the two men duck under cover of the trees.

Everton Conger

The ground thunders with horses' hooves. Everton Conger wipes sweat from his brow. They are close—so very close.

Bowling Green is just ahead. Conger looks up as they pass a dirt lane leading to a lone farmhouse. He urges his horse to go even faster. Clouds of dust rise from the horse's hooves.

He doesn't look back as the dust settles. He doesn't see two men, one with a broken leg, emerge from the woods and make their way back to the farmhouse.

The cavalry reaches the Star Hotel just before midnight. The windows are dark and the door locked. No one inside stirs, despite Everton Conger's pounding. Conger and Edward Doherty make their way to the rear of the hotel and resume their ferocious knocking on the back door. Soon the owner's wife opens it, rubbing her eyes. "Where's Willie Jett?" Conger demands.

The sleepy woman leads them upstairs to a bedroom where Jett lies sleeping. "Get up!" Doherty hollers. "We've got some questions for you."

Downstairs in the parlor, the detectives bark questions at Jett. "If you don't tell us everything you know," one of the detectives warns, "you will suffer!"

Jett looks frightened. He turns to Conger. "I'll talk to you, and you only."

Conger nods and motions for the others to leave the room. His pulse builds with anticipation.

"I'll show ya where Booth is," Jett says. "But under one condition. You gotta make it look like I'm your prisoner. Don't wanna look like I'm helping any Yankees."

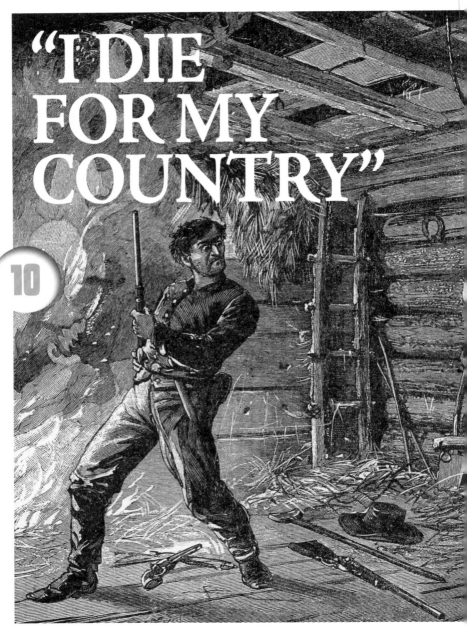

"I DIE FOR MY COUNTRY"

10

Booth refused to surrender without a fight.

John Wilkes Booth,

John Wilkes Booth wakes to a flurry of noises. He blinks, trying to see in the darkness of the tobacco barn, where the Garretts forced him to hide. He hears the noises again. Just farm dogs barking, he realizes. He's about to roll over and go back to sleep when he hears another sound—hooves, hundreds of hooves, rolling across the earth. The sound grows louder and the dogs bark and howl.

Booth shakes Herold awake. "We've got to get out of here," he hisses.

Herold leaps up and grabs his gun, and the two rush to the front of the barn. The door won't budge. "Is it locked?" Herold says, kicking ferociously at the door. "If we can just pry a board free, we could wriggle out."

Booth tries to help, but his injured leg shrieks in pain.

"You'd better surrender," Herold urges as the cavalry thunders into the farmyard.

Booth shakes his head. "Never. I would rather die."

Everton Conger
April 26, Garrett Farm, 2:00 a.m.

Horses neigh as the troops surround the Garrett farmhouse. Luther Baker and Everton Conger jump from their saddles and stride up the porch. Conger hammers on the door with his fists.

Richard Garrett, still in his nightclothes and holding a flickering candle, cracks the door open. "What do you want?"

Baker grabs the old man's shirt and pulls him outside.

"Where are the two men who were here today?" Conger demands.

Garrett looks flustered and confused, still shaking off sleep. "They're … they're in the woods," he stammers.

"Why are they in the woods? Which way did they go?" Conger asks.

The old man shrugs. "I don't know," he says.

"Liar!" barks Baker. "Bring a rope. We'll hang this old rebel." He leans close to Garrett's face. "Unless he wants to talk …"

Garrett stares at them. The candle in his hand shakes. "I—I don't know!" he sputters.

"Hang him!" Baker cries.

John Wilkes Booth

April 26, Garrett Farm, 2:15 a.m.

The barn is surrounded. Booth hears the muffled shouts of the cavalry and the horses' hooves closing in. The end is near. The final act has begun.

The barn door opens and Richard Garrett's son, Jack, stumbles in. "You gotta surrender," he gasps. "Please."

"You filthy scoundrel," Booth growls. "You betrayed me. Get out, or I'll shoot you."

Jack scurries out of the barn, leaving Booth and Herold alone in the darkness.

Booth peers through slats of the barn door. The cavalrymen are so close he can smell their sweat and hear the snorts of their horses. "What do you want?" Booth cries.

"We know who you are!" a voice calls. "Surrender yourselves!"

"Let me think about it," Booth says, stalling for time.

"I'm going," Herold blurts. "I'm surrendering."

Booth whirls on Herold, shocked. Here is a man who has suffered alongside him for twelve days on the run. Now he's trembling like a frightened rabbit and about to run into the arms of the enemy? "You coward!" Booth yells. "Get out. Go!"

With Herold gone, Booth is alone.

"I'm nothing but a cripple," he calls to the cavalry. "Let me out to have a fair fight!"

"No!" yells one of the officers. "Lay down your weapons and surrender."

Cowards! Booth thinks.

"Well, my brave boys," Booth says. He hopes the officers can sense his sarcasm. "Prepare a stretcher for me!"

Everton Conger

A lone man emerges from the barn, his hands up. Conger knows with a glance that it's not Booth.

He looks up at the moon. Only a few hours of darkness remain. Booth could easily shoot from the shelter of the barn. Conger knows that once the sun rises, he and his men will be targets. "We have to act now!" Conger says to Baker.

Just then, a young soldier grabs his arm. It's Boston Corbett, a sergeant. "I'll go in," he says. "I'll fight him one-on-one."

Conger shakes his head. He has a far better plan. He orders the Garretts to gather as much straw as they can and place it against the barn. When they've finished this, he steps forward, match in hand, and sets the hay alight. One corner of the barn catches fire, and the blaze burns bright against the night sky.

Booth will have no choice but to come out now.

John Wilkes Booth

April 26, Garrett Farm, 3:00 a.m.

Booth coughs as smoke fills the barn. The heat is intense, and he feels like his skin is melting. *So that's what they want,* he thinks. *They want me alive, so I can be put on trial and hanged like a common criminal. But I won't give it to them.*

He moves to the front of the barn and leans on one crutch, a rifle against his hip and a revolver in the other hand. He lets the crutch fall to the ground. Slowly, he lifts the rifle.

Everton Conger

The blaze lights up the barn. In the light of the blaze, Conger sees the dark silhouette of the man inside. He sees the man lift his rifle.

A gunshot pierces the air. Booth crumples, his rifle clattering to the ground. Conger doesn't know who fired the shot. But he has to get Booth out of the burning building, dead or alive.

He races into the smoke-filled barn, Baker at his side. They lift Booth and carry him out under the stars.

Booth is alive. As the barn burns, Conger and Baker carry him to the farmhouse porch. In the firelight, Conger sees Booth's lips moving. He bends down to hear what Booth is saying. "Tell my mother I die for my country," Booth whispers.

Conger rises and looks out over the gathered soldiers. "Who fired the shot?" he asks.

Boston Corbett, the young sergeant who offered to go into the barn, steps forward. "I did, sir! He was about to shoot. I had to protect my fellow soldiers."

Conger sighs. Booth is dying. He deserves it, of course, but now any missing pieces of the conspiracy puzzle will die along with him.

John Wilkes Booth
April 26, Garrett Farm, Dawn

Booth can't feel his legs. He can't feel anything. He tries to speak but his voice is only a whisper. "Kill me," he pleads.

The rising sun colors the horizon and shines over Booth's face. He knows he is dying. His throat is swelling, his heart struggling to thump.

"My hands," he croaks.

One of the officers lifts his hands. Booth stares at his paralyzed hands, the same hands that killed Abraham Lincoln. Then he utters his final line: "Useless. Useless."

FAREWELL

Abraham Lincoln's body is placed on the second car of a train that will travel to his hometown of Springfield, Illinois. There, he will be laid to rest.

The train passes through towns and farmland, over hills and across rivers. All across the country, along the train's path, Americans gather to bid farewell to their leader. They tip their hats, bow their heads, and shake with sobs as the train passes.

Southerners are mourning too. Abraham Lincoln wanted to treat the South with respect and compassion. Now their fate lies in the hands of Edwin Stanton and others in the government who want to see the South punished. In the coming years, the South will suffer under the government's harsh policies. John Wilkes Booth, in his attempt to support the South by killing the president, has in fact done more harm than good.

Black Americans, many newly freed from slavery, gather too along the railroad. One man, watching the funeral train rumble into the horizon, calls out, "Farewell, Father Abraham!"

TIMELINE

MARCH 17, 1865

+ Booth's plan to kidnap Lincoln fails.

APRIL 11, 1865

+ Secretary Stanton proposes severe punishment for the South.
+ Lincoln indicates that he wants new rights for black people.
+ Booth decides to assassinate Lincoln rather than kidnap him.

APRIL 14, 1865

+ Mary Lincoln suggests going to Ford's Theatre.
+ Booth discovers Lincoln will be at the theatre.
+ Booth sets his plan in motion by having guns sent to Surratt's tavern in Maryland. He goes to Ford's Theatre to set a piece of wood inside the presidential box so he can wedge the door shut.
+ Dr. Charles Leale discovers the president will be at the play and decides to attend.

10:00–10:30 P.M.

+ Booth enters the theatre and sneaks into the presidential box. He shoots the president, jumps to the stage, and runs out the back door.
+ Dr. Leale rushes to the president's side and declares the wound is fatal, although Lincoln is still alive.

10:30–11:10 P.M.

+ Dr. Leale and others carry Lincoln to the Petersen boardinghouse.
+ Booth escapes Washington, D.C. into Maryland.
+ Stanton assumes control of the government.

APRIL 15, 1865

+ Booth meets Herold, a co-conspirator, and the two travel to Dr. Samuel Mudd's.
+ Stanton interviews eyewitnesses and calls for Booth's arrest.
+ At 7:22 a.m., Lincoln dies.

April 17, 1865

+ Several of Booth's co-conspirators are arrested.

April 20, 1865

+ Booth and Herold cross the Potomac River but end up in Maryland again.

April 21, 1865

+ Dr. Samuel Mudd is questioned.

April 23, 1865

+ Booth and Herold cross the Potomac River into Virginia.
+ Stanton sends the Sixteenth New York Cavalry to Virginia.

April 24, 1865

+ Everton Conger's cavalry searches Virginia for Booth and Herold.
+ Booth and Herold meet Confederate soldiers who take them to Richard Garrett's farm.

April 25, 1865

+ Richard Garrett's son, Jack, becomes suspicious and makes Booth and Herold sleep in a barn.

April 26, 1865

+ Conger learns Booth is at Garrett's farm, and the cavalry race to the farm and surround it.
+ Herold surrenders but Booth refuses.
+ Conger sets fire to the barn to flush Booth out.
+ Booth raises his rifle and a soldier shoots him. He dies in the early morning.

GLOSSARY

assassination (uh-sass-uh-NAY-shun)—the murder of someone who is well known or important

cabinet (KA-buh-nit)—a group of officials who give advice to the president

cavalry (KA-vuhl-ree)—soldiers who travel and fight on horseback

conspiracy (kuhn-SPEER-uh-see)—a secret, illegal plan made by two or more people

pardon (PAHR-duhn)—an act of official forgiveness for a serious offense

telegram (TEL-uh-gram)—a message that is sent by telegraph, a device for sending messages over long distances with electrical signals

tyrant (TYE-ruhnt)—someone who rules other people in a cruel or unjust way

valet (va-LAY)—a person who attends to the personal needs of another person

CRITICAL THINKING USING THE COMMON CORE

1. After the Civil War ended, President Lincoln proposed a reconstruction plan he hoped would heal the country by treating the South kindly. Edwin Stanton and other political figures argued that this approach was wrong. They believed that the Southern states should be punished for their rebellion. Do you think Lincoln's death changed the course of Reconstruction? Why or why not? Use information from the book and other sources to support your answers.
   (Integration of Knowledge and Ideas)

2. John Wilkes Booth and others originally conspired to kidnap Lincoln and make an exchange for Confederate prisoners-of-war. But the plot became focused on assassination after Booth heard the president deliver a speech. What factors contributed to the evolution of the plot? Support your answer using information from at least two other texts or valid Internet sources.
   (Key Ideas and Details)

INTERNET SITES

FactHound offers a safe, fun way to find Internet sites related to this book. All of the sites on FactHound have been researched by our staff.

Here's all you do:
Visit www.facthound.com
Type in this code: 9781491470763

FactHound will fetch the best sites for you!

FURTHER READING

Fitzgerald, Stephanie. *Reconstruction: Rebuilding America after the Civil War.* North Mankato, Minn.: Compass Point Books, 2011.

Holzer, Harold. *Father Abraham: Lincoln and His Sons.* Honesdale, Pa.: Calkins Creek, 2010.

Nardo, Don. *The Presidency of Abraham Lincoln: The Triumph of Freedom and Unity.* North Mankato, Minn.: Compass Point Books, 2015.

Otfinoski, Steven. *Yankees and Rebels: Stories of U.S. Civil War Leaders.* North Mankato, Minn.: Capstone Press, 2015.

Swanson, James L. *Chasing Lincoln's Killer.* New York: Scholastic Press, 2009.

SELECTED BIBLIOGRAPHY

Axelrod, Alan. *Lincoln's Last Night: Abraham Lincoln, John Wilkes Booth, and the Last 36 Hours Before the Assassination.* New York: Chamberlain Brothers, 2005.

Goodman, Barak. *American Experience. The Assassination of Abraham Lincoln.* Arlington, Va.: PBS Home Video, 2009.

Larson, Kate Clifford. *The Assassin's Accomplice: Mary Surratt and the Plot to Kill Abraham Lincoln.* New York: MJF Books, 2012.

O'Reilly, Bill and Martin Dugard. *Killing Lincoln: The Shocking Assassination that Changed America Forever.* New York: Henry Holt and Co., 2011.

Steers, Edward. *Blood on the Moon: The Assassination of Abraham Lincoln.* Lexington, Ky.: University Press of Kentucky, 2001.

Steers, Edward. *The Lincoln Assassination Encyclopedia.* New York: Harper Perennial, 2010.

Steers, Edward and Harold Holzer, eds. *The Lincoln Assassination Conspirators: Their Confinement and Execution, As Recorded in the Letterbook of John Frederick Hartranft.* Baton Rouge, La.: Louisiana State University Press, 2009.

Swanson, James L. and Daniel R. Weinberg. *Lincoln's Assassins: Their Trial and Execution: An Illustrated History.* New York: W. Morrow, 2006.

INDEX

Arnold, Samuel, 10, 12, 15, 81
Atzerodt, George, 10, 12, 42, 43, 65
Baker, Luther, 87, 91, 98, 99, 101, 103
Conger, Everton, 87, 89–90, 91–92, 94–95, 98–99, 101, 103–104
Corbett, Boston, 101, 104
Cox, Samuel, 79, 82
Davis, Jefferson, 28
Doherty, Edward, 87, 94, 95
Garrett, Richard, 91, 92, 97, 98, 99, 101
Grant, Ulysses S., 17, 22, 25, 26, 27, 29, 31, 33, 34, 35, 73
Harris, Clara, 40, 45, 51
Hawk, Harry, 48, 56, 57, 59
Herold, David, 10, 42, 43, 64–65, 71, 72, 74, 75, 76, 77, 82, 83, 85, 86, 87, 88, 89, 90, 93, 97, 98, 99, 100
Jett, Willie, 90–91, 92, 93, 94–95
Johnson, Andrew, 31, 43, 65
Keene, Laura, 26, 47
Leale, Charles, 20–21, 33, 46–47, 59, 61–62, 69, 72, 75–76

Lee, Robert E., 17, 25, 27
Lincoln, Mary Todd, 13–14, 25–26, 32–33, 36, 40, 45–46, 51, 57, 58, 61–62, 69, 75
Lincoln, Robert, 25, 69
Lincoln, Tad, 19, 25
Lincoln, Willie, 32
Lovett, Alexander, 84–85, 87
Lucas, William, 86, 87
Mudd, Samuel, 74–75, 77, 79, 82, 84–85
O'Laughlen, Michael, 10, 12, 81
Peanuts, John, 48, 59
Powell, Lewis, 10, 42–43, 65, 80–81
Rathbone, Henry, 40, 45, 58
Rollins, William, 88, 91–92
Seward, William, 31, 41, 42–43, 63, 64–65, 66, 67, 72, 80, 81
Stanton, Edwin, 17–18, 28–29, 41, 63, 66–67, 70, 73, 76, 80–81, 85, 87, 105
Stuart, Richard, 79, 86
Surratt, John, 10
Surratt, Mary, 31, 71, 80, 81
Welles, Gideon, 66, 67
Wells, Henry, 84, 85, 87

ABOUT THE AUTHOR

Jessica Gunderson grew up in the small town of Washburn, North Dakota. She has a bachelor's degree from the University of North Dakota and an MFA in Creative Writing from Minnesota State University, Mankato. She has written more than fifty books for young readers. Her book *Ropes of Revolution* won the 2008 Moonbeam Award for best graphic novel. She currently lives in Madison, Wisconsin, with her husband and cat.